ZOO ANIMALS

Penguins

Debbie Gallagher

Marshall Cavendish
Benchmark
New York

This edition first published in 2010 in the United States of America by Marshall Cavendish Benchmark
An imprint of Marshall Cavendish Corporation

All rights reserved.

No part of this publication may be reproduced, stored in a retrieval system or transmitted, in any form or by any means, electronic, mechanical, photocopying, recording, or otherwise, without the prior permission of the copyright owner. Request for permission should be addressed to the Publisher, Marshall Cavendish Corporation, 99 White Plains Road, Tarrytown, NY 10591. Tel: (914) 332-8888, fax: (914) 332-1888.

Website: www.marshallcavendish.us

This publication represents the opinions and views of the author based on Debbie Gallagher's personal experience, knowledge, and research. The information in this book serves as a general guide only. The author and publisher have used their best efforts in preparing this book and disclaim liability rising directly and indirectly from the use and application of this book.

Other Marshall Cavendish Offices:
Marshall Cavendish Ltd. 5th Floor, 32-38 Saffron Hill, London EC1N 8 FH, UK • Marshall Cavendish International (Asia) Private Limited, 1 New Industrial Road, Singapore 536196 • Marshall Cavendish International (Thailand) Co Ltd. 253 Asoke, 12th Flr, Sukhumvit 21 Road, Klongtoey Nua, Wattana, Bangkok 10110, Thailand • Marshall Cavendish (Malaysia) Sdn Bhd, Times Subang, Lot 46, Subang Hi-Tech Industrial Park, Batu Tiga, 40000 Shah Alam, Selangor Darul Ehsan, Malaysia

Marshall Cavendish is a trademark of Times Publishing Limited

All websites were available and accurate when this book was sent to press.

Library of Congress Cataloging-in-Publication Data

Gallagher, Debbie, 1969-
  Penguins / Debbie Gallagher.
     p. cm. — (Zoo animals)
  Includes index.
  Summary: "Discusses penguins, their natural habitat, behavior, characteristics, and zoo life"—Provided by publisher.
  ISBN 978-0-7614-4747-4
  1. Captive penguins—Juvenile literature. 2. Penguins—Juvenile literature. 3. Zoo animals—Juvenile literature. I. Title.
  SF473.P46G35 2010
  636.6—dc22
                              2009040077

First published in 2010 by
MACMILLAN EDUCATION AUSTRALIA PTY LTD
15–19 Claremont Street, South Yarra 3141

Visit our website at www.macmillan.com.au or go directly to www.macmillanlibrary.com.au

Associated companies and representatives throughout the world.

Copyright © Debbie Gallagher 2010

Edited by Georgina Garner
Text and cover design by Kerri Wilson
Page layout by Raul Diche
Photo research by Legend Images
Base maps by Gaston Vanzet, modified by Kerri Wilson

Printed in the United States

Acknowledgments
The author and the publisher are grateful to the following for permission to reproduce copyright material:

Front cover photo of Gentoo penguin feeding chicks © James Richey/iStockphoto

Photographs courtesy of: AAP/AP Photo/Renzo Gostoli, 20; AAP/AP Photo/Ricardo Moraes, 21; Pattie Anderson, 27 (left); Jeremy Eades, 13; Bruno Gerber, 16; © Yaromyr Babskyy/iStockphoto, 12; © James Richey/iStockphoto, 1, 19; © Thomas Shortell/iStockphoto, 10; © yaxxcom/iStockphoto, 4; Knoxville Zoo, 30; Legendimages, 24, 25, 26 (right); Loro Parque, 3, 22, 26 (left), 28, 29; Marwell Zoological Park, 14, 15; © Raimund Linke/Masterfile, 18; Andrew McColl, 17; Oregon Zoo, photo by Michael Durham, 23; Penguins-Eastern Cape, www.penguin-rescue.org.za, 11; Photolibrary/Donna Ikenberry 7; Saint Louis Zoo, 27 (right); © Avalon Imaging/Shutterstock, 6; © jgl247/Shutterstock, 8 (penguin silhouette); © Shironina/Shutterstock, 5.

Many zoos helped in the creation of this book. The authors would especially like to thank ZooParc de Beauval, France, Loro Parque Zoo, Tenerife, Marwell Zoological Park, England, Penguins-Eastern Cape, South Africa, Saint Louis Zoo, USA, Oregon Zoo, USA, Knoxville Zoo, USA, and The Royal Zoological Society of Scotland, Edinburgh Zoo, Scotland.

While every care has been taken to trace and acknowledge copyright, the publisher tenders their apologies for any accidental infringement where copyright has proved untraceable. Where the attempt has been unsuccessful, the publisher welcomes information that would redress the situation.

1 3 5 6 4 2

Contents

Zoos	4
Penguins	6
In the Wild	8
Zoo Homes	12
Zoo Food	14
Zoo Health	16
Baby Penguins	18
How Zoos Are Saving Penguins	20
Meet Benoît, a Penguin Keeper	24
A Day in the Life of a Zookeeper	26
Zoos Around the World	28
The Importance of Zoos	30
Glossary	31
Index	32

When a word is printed in **bold**, you can look up its meaning in the Glossary on page 31.

Zoos

Zoos are places where people can see a lot of different animals. The animals in a zoo come from all around the world.

People can visit zoos to see animals from other parts of the world.

Zoos have special **enclosures** for each different type of animal. Some enclosures are like the animals' homes in the **wild**. They have trees for climbing and water for swimming.

Animals from cold places, such as polar bears, need cold temperatures in their enclosures.

Penguins

Penguins are birds. They cannot fly but they are excellent swimmers. They spend most of their lives swimming in the sea. Penguins have black and white **waterproof** feathers.

- black and white feathers
- flipper-like wings
- webbed feet

A penguin's body is suited to its life on land and in water.

There are seventeen different **species** of penguins. Some have colorful beaks or brightly colored feathers on their head. Emperor penguins are the largest. Little penguins are the smallest species.

Rockhopper penguins have brightly colored feathers that look like long eyebrows.

In the Wild

In the wild, penguins only live in the southern half of the world, called the Southern Hemisphere. They live on land beside the sea.

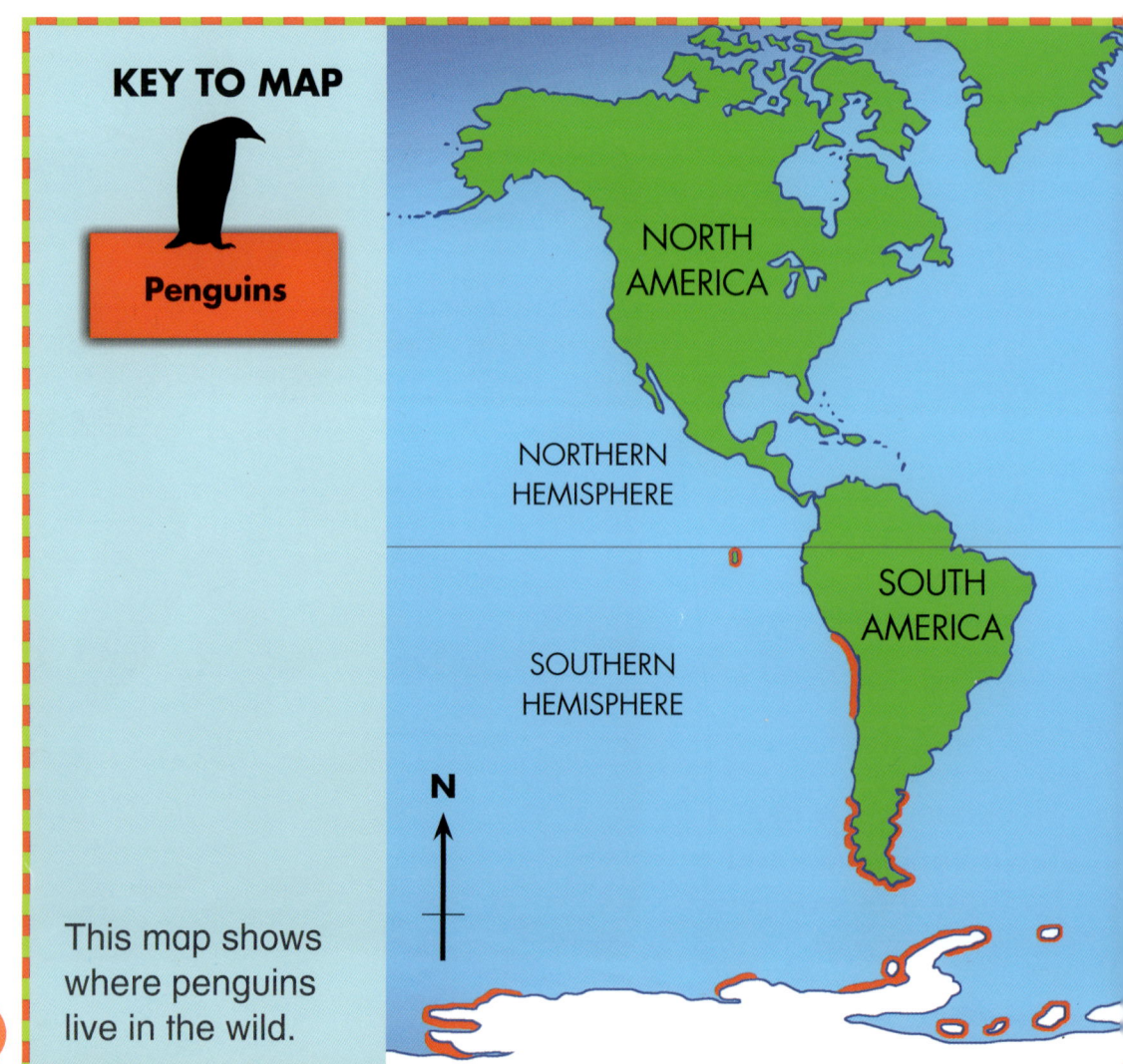

This map shows where penguins live in the wild.

Penguins build nests and **burrows** on land in large groups, called colonies. They swim in the sea to find food, such as fish and **krill**.

Threats to Survival

The biggest threat to the survival of penguins is fishing. Large **trawlers** catch the fish that the penguins need to eat. Some penguins are injured or killed by fishing nets.

Trawlers use strong, wide fishing nets to catch fish.

Trawlers and other ships **pollute** the sea when they dump water from their fuel tanks. This water has oil mixed in it. The oil kills penguins and other sea life.

A penguin that is covered in oil is unable to swim properly.

Zoo Homes

In zoos, penguins live in enclosures. These enclosures are built like the penguins' **habitats** in the wild. Some enclosures have rocks, sand, and pools of water.

- burrows for nesting
- rock
- pool of water

This penguin enclosure has a rocky beach and nesting burrows.

Penguins from cold areas need cold air and water in their enclosures. Penguins from warmer areas, such as Humboldt penguins, prefer warm air, rocks, and sand.

burrows for nesting

snow

King penguins need cold air and snow in their enclosures.

Zoo Food

Zoos feed penguins the same food that they eat in the wild. Zookeepers add vitamins and minerals to the food to keep the penguins healthy.

Some zoos use an underwater penguin feeder.

A Penguin's Zoo Food
fish, such as anchovies, sardines, and herring
squid
krill
shrimp

Feeding

Many zoos have a special time each day when visitors can watch the penguins eat. Zookeepers often hand-feed the penguins to make sure each one gets enough food.

A zookeeper hand-feeds the penguins.

Zoo Health

Penguins need to exercise so that they stay healthy. Zookeepers sometimes take penguins on walks around the zoo. The penguins get some exercise and see new sights.

Penguins take a walk around a zoo.

Zoos have **veterinarians,** or vets, who look after sick penguins. Vets also give advice to zookeepers about keeping penguins healthy.

A vet and zookeeper check a sick penguin.

Baby Penguins

Baby penguins, called chicks, come from eggs. Mother penguins lay one or two eggs at a time. The mother and father usually take care of the eggs and chicks.

An emperor penguin keeps its chick warm.

The parents bring food back to the nest for their chicks. Chicks need to grow waterproof feathers before they can swim and catch their own food.

A penguin gives a chick food from its own stomach.

How Zoos Are Saving Penguins

Niterói Zoo in Brazil saves lost and sick penguins. Each year, hundreds of young penguins are washed up on Brazil's beaches. The penguins come from colder areas in the south.

These penguins were rescued from Brazil's beaches and taken to Niterói Zoo.

Workers at the Niterói Zoo take care of the injured and sick penguins. When the penguins become stronger, they are brought back to their homes in the wild.

A vet at Niterói Zoo takes care of a rescued penguin.

Zoos Working Together

Zoos often share animals for **breeding**. Baby animals are healthiest when their parents are from different family groups. Mother and father penguins from different zoos make healthy chicks.

Penguins are placed in special boxes before traveling to a new zoo for breeding.

Oregon Zoo keeps a record of the parents of its penguins. This information is helpful when it shares the penguins for breeding.

A vet checks the health of a baby penguin bred at Oregon Zoo.

Meet Benoît, a Penguin Keeper

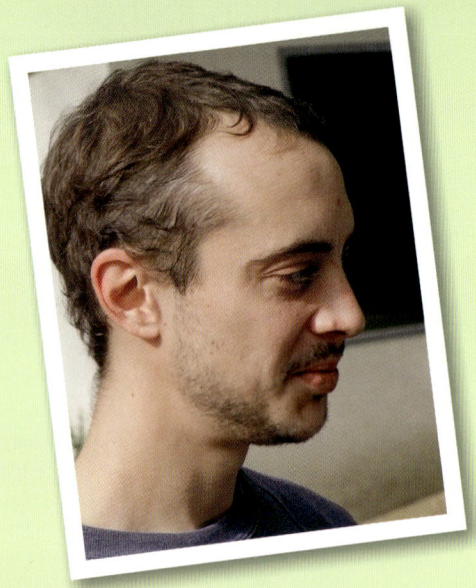

Benoît works as a zookeeper in France.

Question	Why did you become a zookeeper?
Answer	I have always wanted to work with birds.
Question	How long have you been a zookeeper?
Answer	I have worked in zoos for four years.

Benoît throws fish to the penguins.

Question   What animals have you worked with?

Answer   I have worked with penguins, parrots, eagles, and monkeys.

Question   What do you like about your job?

Answer   I especially like being able to discover new ways to improve the lives of zoo birds.

A Day in the Life of a Zookeeper

Zookeepers have jobs to do every day. Often, a team of zookeepers work together to look after the penguins at a zoo.

8:00 a.m.
Clean the penguin enclosure.

9:00 a.m.
Prepare fish and weigh food for the day.

1:30 p.m.
Check penguins are healthy and happy.

3:30 p.m.
Feed fish to the penguins.

Zoos Around the World

Loro Parque Zoo is in Tenerife, in Spain. The zoo has king, rockhopper, gentoo, and chinstrap penguins. These penguins need cold temperatures.

Loro Parque is home to gentoo penguins.

The temperature in the zoo's "Planet Penguin" enclosure is freezing. Snow falls into the enclosure from machines in the roof. King penguins slide on their bellies over the snow.

"Planet Penguin," at Loro Parque Zoo, is a snowy island surrounded by cold water.

The Importance of Zoos

Zoos do very important work. They:
- help people learn about animals
- save **endangered** animals and animals that are badly treated

Knoxville Zoo, in Tennessee, is helping save African penguins.

Glossary

breeding — Caring for animals so that they can produce babies.

burrows — Holes where animals live or sleep.

enclosures — The fenced-in areas where animals are kept in zoos.

endangered — At high risk of dying out and disappearing from Earth.

habitats — Areas in which animals are naturally found.

krill — Tiny, shelled animals that live in the sea.

pollute — To poison or make dirty.

species — Groups of animals or plants that have similar features.

trawlers — Ships that catch fish by dragging a strong, wide net through the sea.

veterinarians — Animal doctors.

waterproof — Keeping out water.

wild — Natural areas, such as forests, that are untouched by humans.

Index

a
animal health, 14, 16–17, 22, 23, 27

b
baby animals, 18–19, 22, 23
breeding, 22, 23
burrows, 9, 12, 13

c
chinstrap penguins, 28

e
emperor penguins, 7, 18
enclosures, 5, 12–13, 26

f
fishing trawlers, 10, 11
food, 9, 14–15, 19, 26, 27

g
gentoo penguins, 28

h
habitats, 12
Humboldt penguins, 13

k
king penguins, 13, 28, 29

l
little penguins, 7
Loro Parque Zoo, 28, 29

n
nests, 9, 19
Niterói Zoo, 20, 21

o
Oregon Zoo, 23

p
pollution, 11

r
rescued penguins, 20, 21
rockhopper penguins, 7, 28

t
threats to survival, 10–11

v
veterinarians, 17, 21, 23

w
wild animals, 5, 8–9

z
zookeepers, 14, 15, 16, 17, 24–5, 26–7
zoo projects, 22–3